# BOOK REVIEWS

1. *"A 15- year old wordsmith! A remarkable young talent! That's Shaina. I have witnessed her transformation from a hesitant speaker in 2019 to a captivating leader who inspires others. Her sheer determination propelled her onto the stage as she now confidently guides Gavel club members, her infectious enthusiasm and unwavering support empowering them to find their own voices. She's a testament to the power of personal growth, a firebrand who lights the ways for others. I was extremely happy when she told me about this poetry book, knowing her taste, I felt a thrill of anticipation. Could this be the missing piece I have been searching for in my own bookshelf? I found out this collection of poems, a mirror reflecting the myriad facets of her character, speaks volumes of truth. It's her thoughts, emotions, and observations about the world around her. Through her lens, the world refracts, revealing secrets whispered from realms beyond. Her authenticity, her unfiltered voice cracks open hearts, weaving threads of raw truth that bind readers like whispers in the darkness. It is her attitude that breathes life into these pages. Her curiosity is boundless, her sense of wonder infectious. She navigates the complexities of adolescence with a grace that is both admirable and enviable. Through her poetry, with each poem she sculpts empathy from the raw clay of language, forging connections that resonate*

*in the depths of every soul. My heartfelt wishes to Shaina. May her inkwell spill with endless verses, may her poems forever dance on the tongues of generations, a testament to the power of words to heal and to uplift."*

**Mr. Ajith Perera**
*Counselor - Dubai Gavel Club*
*Toastmasters International*
*Chairman Group I*
*Global Youth Gavel Clubs*

2. *"If one can immerse themselves in a bouquet of senses, it would be when they are reading this anthology of poems by this young poet Shaina Mukherjee. Each poem is written with complete honesty, baring the feelings that still seek maturity of the experienced, but nevertheless written in a highly inspiring manner. As I read the variety of thoughts presented in verse, I could delve into an incredible depth of wisdom. Some poems are powerful and insightful in their totality. They explore deeply the multiple sides of polarizing human nature. If we look closer at the verse-forms, we will notice that many poems are not divided into stanzas, it is ongoing. We can assume that this can illustrate the concept that life is flowing without breaks and every moment of life captured through the poets' senses contributes to the whole. Shaina as a poet portrays the facets of human life, stirs emotions and leaves us thoughtful. I keep wondering if I hear the poet's voice. Is the poet sharing her life experiences throughout the poems? But keeping that aside, I do hear a speaker's voice, invisible throughout all of Shaina's poems. Despite the poet's use of first person throughout, her voice is invisible. The allure of being told without being told! This is a powerful approach,*

*which helps in drawing the audience's attention as it draws mine."*

**Dr. Chitra Raghavan**

<u>*Vice-Principal Academics- Delhi Private School, Sharjah*</u>
<u>*Educator, Trainer, Freelance writer*</u>

3. *"Great job! May this be the first of many. God Bless! Best wishes."*

**Mrs. Vandana Marwaha**

<u>*Principal and Director of Delhi Private School, Sharjah*</u>

Shaina Mukherjee is currently a grade 10 student at DPS, Sharjah. This is her first published book, Venture, which she began writing as a 13-year-old doing her eighth grade. Although she proved her mettle both in academics and extracurriculars, indulging in versatile arenas, reading and writing have always been her greatest passion and strength, which eventually guided her to take up leadership roles in school over the years, consecutively as house captain, president-editorial and editorial coordinator. She had also been a voracious gavelier for the past four years of Dubai Gavel Club (an affiliate of Toastmasters International), currently serving as the vice president of education, undertaking responsibilities such as mentoring, planning, and organizing and meeting the educational needs of each member. In the year 2020–21, she held the position of vice president of public relations at the club. Over the years, she has exhibited exemplary skills and won several inter- and intra-club speech contests.

There is always that one person whose sole purpose and dedication in life is to see you smile. Although I have four cheerleaders in my life, namely my mother (Mamma), father (Baba), maternal grandmother (Didai) and maternal uncle (Bhaimama), the most enthusiastic one has to be my maternal grandmother, Tripti Chakraborty. Her whole life, she has always put everybody above herself and as her only granddaughter, I would like to put the spotlight on her just this once, in my mini-feat. Didai, as I affectionately address her, irrespective of the fact that you are physically miles away from me, I will always carry you in the deepest foundation of my soul. No number of words can express my undying love for you. You have always been there for me, in body and soul. You have shown me such unconditional love that only a few people get the chance to experience.

Shaina Mukherjee

# 40 PEARLS OF A TEEN

AUSTIN MACAULEY PUBLISHERS™
LONDON • CAMBRIDGE • NEW YORK • SHARJAH

ISBN – 9789948775843 – (Paperback)
ISBN – 9789948775836 – (E-Book)

Application Number: MC-10-01-6014890
Age Classification: E

First Published 2024
AUSTIN MACAULEY PUBLISHERS FZE
Sharjah Publishing City
P.O Box [519201]
Sharjah, UAE
www.austinmacauley.ae
+971 655 95 202

Throughout my meagre 15 years of existence, the two people to always care, correct and celebrate me, irrespective of the hurdles I constantly challenge them with, are my parents, Tamasree Chakraborty and Saikat Mukherjee, my mamma and baba, respectively.

Thank you, Mamma, for everything. I cannot really express my gratitude in words, much less in one sentence, but I hope you can grasp the essence of my message. Thank you for being my rock and the bestest friend of mine. Most importantly, thank you for being the only bosom to cry on and the loudest one to cheer amongst the crowd.

Thank you, Baba, for being the goofiest and the most loving father. Although you don't express it much, I know you love me to the moon and back and so do I. Thank you for always being on my side through thick and thin. I will forever cherish your affection and appreciate you for everything you have provided me with and I mean not just the materialistic ones.

My acknowledgements seem incomplete without thanking "destiny and obstacles". Thank you for showing up in this journey until now. Had you not presented yourself, I would have never persuaded myself to explore this side of mine, and hence, this book would never have been written.

Last but not the least thank you, dear reader, for picking up this book and giving it a chance. Because that's what life's all about, really. GIVING CHANCES!!!

# Table of Contents

# **<u>Building the Broken</u>**

Incapacity, inability, an array of words,
Promptly used without a second thought,
But once they descend down upon us,
Haa! Look at those frowning odds.
Viewed as rays of misfortune,
Trashed and belittled upon
are such adversities,
But those shades that you fail to remove,
arc the ones obstructing you to view
the rays of light shining upon you.
Surges of primal energy,
Flow through you,
Parts of you seemingly weak,
Become stronger than ever,
Young sprogs, such an inspiration,
The experienced fails to see,
The more you break, the harder your pillars will be!
Words are at a loss, for those scenes,
Playing out in theatrical obscene,
Unfathomable is the power of you,
the supposed glass inside shatters,
Yet a pillar of steel builds in you.

Misunderstood are the afflictions of pain indeed,
Open your eyes, look around and see,
The pain that blinds you,
Also creates the vital vibes within that keeps resounding within you timelessly!

# Whirling Sandstorm

The dusty wind whines a mournful tune,
As the dry drought prickles the crystalline lagoon,
Shriveling and withering within those blistering hues,
Lies a spesh treasure, waiting to be unveiled,
Oh, would it be as desirable as the misty dews?
But how to uncover its site, a ghost in its customary form,
When it wants to hide, fancies to scorn,
Hallelujah! I have the key up my torn sleeve,
A way to find a ghost that hides in the shadows of grief,
Show a torch, o lil' sprog and you'll see the lost gold,
Shimmering its light through the hazy brown skies.
What good will gold do to the heat,
What good will its shine do to the sun's glazing burn,
What good shall its worth do to the quenching of the thirst,
Sham it was all this time, scouring through the dirt and mud!
Rage engulfs the clear sight; oh, I wasted a day and night!
Bleeding foot, bitten by the scorpions of greed,
Lured by desire,
Oh, you veiled beauty, show your true self,
For you have brought misfortune

She descends in her divine ingress,
As she smirks, laughs and bellows,
"You fool, I brought you out of the lushy lagoons,
So you can taste the sight of your own petty soul!"

# Alluring Scent

Solace, we often seek,
A shoulder to lean on and pacify yourself,
A handy bucket to pour the pain out,
A mighty syringe to suck the agony up,
Oh, jaunty tools men, lend your instruments already!
When four out of five senses go numb,
You are left with only one,
Toiling with your reliant nose,
Sniffing out a comforting source.
Ah, that familiar rosy scent,
Muffled with that dearly mouthwatering gourmet,
You sprint young one,
Never again you'll trace that perfume,
No matter how hard you weep or fume!
Cherish that softness,
Those whispers and murmurs of loftiness,
Wise words you may never hear from another,
Oh, why I bother to look for another her?
That hearty bosom of mine,
Kindred one I shall always look for,
There is only perfume I smell on her,
That's what I remember when I ponder on her.

# **<u>Weather Swap</u>**

The gloom in the sky,
hangs around like a melancholy dust in the high,
The sun shines it's beaming light,
And sends them off in a scurrying fright,
Weeping trickling tears,
Running sprinting fears,
Oh, why is there so much grey?
As the misty air starts to cloud,
the jovial heat starts to frown,
As melancholy hues,
Start to sing a soothing tune,
the wind picks up their pace,
And rush through leaves in a sprightly haste,
We see yonder tears of rain,
Starting to pour in dire pain.
As the scorching sun,
Shines its blinding light,
the blooming spring starts to cower away in fright,
As the sizzling sparks through the cracks of land,
The dry lands cackles an eerie laugh,
Give no water away to those poor nomads,
We see distant beaming sun,

Glow over so brightly, and it's no fun!
Don't make your life a color-blind lie!
Add a splash of violet, a dash of red,
And a little bit of rainbow in between.

# Becoming Ancient

Tick-tock, click-clock, there goes the repeated chiming,
its constant pursuit in life,
Time, oh time, what a funny lad,
Got a fine taste of humor,
and certainly, it's no rumor!
Playing us like pawns in its game,
Yet it declines any request of fame,
The dust keeps collecting,
As a souvenir to be neglected.
Like a rusty hinge,
We keep falling in the pit of decay,
The increase in hair, so very grey,
The hips are so very immobile, cannot even sway!
When the eyelids flutter close with a droopy look,
Or you are being a bore with a primitive book,
Is your battery charge finally up,
A question that is sprung quite frequently, huff!

# Invisible

All the chatter going about,
The pinging of phones on silent mode,
With no one to look at that frowning face,
The spotlight been shone on you,
What a glory, a moment of no blue!
Yet the microphone malfunctions,
Setting you to silence, well! How rude!
With a speech in hand,
You step up on that wondrous stage,
Yet no light beams on you,
Cannot speak again and furious with rage!
So, no matter what you do,
You should be sitting in the settings room,
As with no light or speaker,
Your speech and you are sure to be doomed!

# Caged Heart

Surrounded by the crowd's hues and cries,
Lies a lonely lass, with keen eyes,
Her eyes flood with tears,
As she's judged by all,
Despite her tries,
to meet the world's expectation of her.
She is blamed for being herself
As nature seems to define itself with all its might,
When she wishes to disappear,
the ground oozes with pointed fingers,
As she whimpers,
With a tattered heart,
She realizes,
She has a caged heart!
The heart tries with all its might,
To break free from the rusty chains,
Bound they are to the unbreaking walls,
Oh, her fate,
Such a shame!
Her tears are her only respite,
She scours through the hazy mirror,
Being the only portal to see herself,

Labelled across with the words they say,
Alas! Finds nothing,
But just another girl,
Hidden in plain sight!

# Horizon

O' you lonely heart,
Look beyond the borders of the horizon,
Where the sun kisses the mighty crust,
And the blazing sun's reflection could be seen at the corner of
your eyes,
Open them wider and you shall find,
A door with a hidden key,
The key is there in the depths of your soul,
I shall give you a hint,
So you may seek it soon,
It is what shall make your face flutter and flush,
Should a boundless horizon come and tickle your heart,
O' indeed it is love, you tender-hearted dear
Rush to that door and witness a whole new world
Without a trickle of fear!

# Lifeline

Hey, you little bird,

Seek pleasure in what you can devour through your eyes,

For it may end in flames,

Any moment whence the funeral pyre is ablaze.

O' you serene beauty,

Do not be vain of your possession,

For the view may distort,

As rain pours upon your reflection,

As dawn begins to set on thee,

Look around and see,

Every living soul's lifetime,

because one leaves this Earth,

Not with a beating heart,

But with the memory of only one's lifetime!

# A Rare Recognition

As the little baby whines in the
loving arms of his new mama,
Everyone turns around,
to gauge her inability to
care for her snug one.
As the kindergarten newbie refuses to
leave his mother's affectionate arms,
Everyone judges her incapacity to raise
a well-mannered one,
As the stubborn teen denies to obey,
his mother's loving ways,
everyone ponders on how poor her raising methods were!
So you see, no matter how hard she tries,
Her maternal efforts, love and care,
Are never appreciated!
Her only recognition comes along
when her little one stands in the real game of life!

# Street Rat

Seated upon a tattered mat,
lies a whimpering street rat,
as his tummy broke into loud growls,
all passed by without a second glance.
On a day as ordinary as the previous,
crosses a beauty enchanting her fellow admirers.
No different than the others,
the insignificant one looks up to her,
only to see her doing the same,
But this pretty moment got shattered in a second,
By a loud interrupting sound.
What is that sound? Where is its origin?
…got deduced in a minute,
by a second glance upon his pale face.
But this time with a little added blush,
As all picked and mocked the poor soul,
The kind Cinderella stood up to all,
Only to hear the cries of her anger roar,
"You nasty ones shall never understand,
The excruciating pain of a little street rat!"

# <u>Struggles</u>

Lying on the street side,
Is a penurious soul impetrating for fundamental needs,
One such passerby looks upon,
Pitying his plight,
Only to think on,
Everyone has their own struggles whatsoever…
As the well-attired gentlemen walked up to his house,
It's seen in a scruffy state,
an antique landline at the corner,
seemed to ring instantly upon his arrival,
As he reaches out to pick up,
It is overheard that the other is agitated to his peak,
The boss unimpressed,
Can make out whimpers from the poor clerk, so distressed.
Pitifully listening, the boss hangs up,
only to lend ears to the screeches of his wife,
As the bigwig descends the stairs,
of his elegant abode,
He thinks to himself,
Everyone has their own struggles whatsoever,
Upon arrival as the affluent employer,
Retorts to his wife,

It is heard that she states something quite not right,
"Invisible I am indeed!"
As she mutters despairingly,
Everyone has their own struggles whatsoever.
This unfortunate chain could reach no length,
Because rightly so…
Everyone has their own struggles whatsoever!

# Identity

Trotted a young chap,
Pride by his side,
Strutting with a shine,
Soon interruption strikes,
Its origin from a wise old man,
Offers the one,
To choose between right and wrong,
Wrong emerges the winner between the two,
But soon the young soul faces his foe,
Battle against his faith,
proved to be tough,
He seemed to reach the end,
With no luck,
But hope prevailed within his heart,
and a winner is revealed,
Its identity is the one,
who right the wrong,
His faith or anything you may name it as,
seems to be the undefeatable one,
to the common eye!

# **<u>Allurement</u>**

In a tiny little town,
lived a group of girlies,
Who worshipped an elegant gown,
Rumored to possess powers,
That anybody could imagine
Trapped it was in a Pandora's box,
And could only be opened by time as it passed,
But impatience creeped into their hearts,
and it smirked peering over the clouds to watch,
The girls soon slipped into the room,
And as all stories do,
One little soul was with the light but alone.
As the box opened,
It was seen in the mirrors formed by those girlies' eyes,
Laid was a filthy, rotten unkempt gown!
Realizing that they unleashed demons in doing so
They sprint to lord-knows-where, but surely afar as it was
believed so!
From a distance, we observed that young little beauty,
Who was singular in her journey,

Determined not to succumb,
Rejoicing in her own divine glow,
Which is often called a "halo"!

# By Force

Expectations of the world,
seems impossible to bear,
When someone else aspires for you,
To go against your will,
Resentment creeps in your heart,
Do not let it poison your inner being
As the world then shall emerge
as the winner of the silent battle,
And grandly rejoice,
at your unwillingly made choice,
Do not show the obedient side of you,
As there are still a few,
Counting on you,
To voice out that t-i-g-e-r within you!

# <u>Voice</u>

Cries and whimpers of a young elegance are shut out,
By the bellowings of an aristocratic man with a beastly frown.
Rewinding her life's tragedy to a few years back,
We witness that,
Her journey had been very rough,
And so had been her surroundings,
so very tough,
All she desired in her life,
Was to live in peace,
As a hermit would do,
But as soon as she opened her door,
with a gleaming shine,
It transformed into a whimpering whine,
Her father raged at her with a foul smile,
"A burden surely you are!"

# Time

Consent proves to be crucial,
For the law, your bills and your wills,
But what about the game you are in life?
The world races as fast as our F1 cars,
It stops for nobody and none
Wanting everything to be at once done,
Everyone battling to get the spotlight,
In a spiffy way,
The understanding deceives,
We are but slaves to time,
and don't realize, this rushy life is cryptic in its game!

# The Reveal

Battered heart, falling apart,
Support weighs nothing now,
Pressure keeps building on,
but does anybody look back?
H-u-h! Not their fault though.
Confessions spurting out,
the truth refuses to core out,
Stabbing the fleshy barrier,
Only seems to make it more harder,
Ohh! You have the guts to cook up a lie?
But not the one to serve,
Oh, you h-y-p-o-c-r-i-t-e,
Reflect back,
Because karma gets back to everyone
and spares almost none!

# <u>Decision</u>

Choices, so volatile,
don't seem to be so vile,
but when the time comes to make one,
Do they put up a show of daggers and knives on one
and daisies and roses on the other!
But what they are concealing,
We may never know!
Youth and old alike,
Seems baffled all the time,
why spend so much time deciphering,
none shall ever acknowledge!
Serving all options on the golden platter,
Shall at the end,
Never make a difference,
In the sufferings of the phenomenon of dilemma!

# Tides, Waves or the Maiden?

When the tides of love crash ashore,
Does the often ignored
attempt to convey the oozing of hatred?
Unable to stand the instability,
Causing a tsunami to stir…!
Whence the encaptivating sea maiden arises
Does the shunned seem to awaken?
The shore exclaims,
Only a young one can quieten the roars of love!
An emotion so very eruptive,
Easily confused with abhor,
Here comes the denial,
A common key to a couple of penned tales,
So very intense,
Like salt and sugar mixed together,
But someone like her,
Can spot the distinct difference,
And tune the waves' rage to a sweet melody!

# Nurture

As giggles and chuckles are heard from the blossoming home,
The beholders send glares,
Muttering strings of colorful words along the way,
Dissatisfied we all are,
By the missing pieces of the puzzle named family,
But forget to cherish the ones that are still there,
As they may too be gone,
By the very next minute,
Whence they'll be buried six feet down,
Don't shed the salty liquid,
That begin to bleed as soon as they go,
Instead cherish the time as long as you have,
And walk them out to the gate of bliss,
As they depart this aureate world!

# The Appealing Blossom

Buzzing bees,
Blooming flowers,
All the waves washing ashore,
Seems to be with the whisk of a wand,
Yet, we want to venture beyond,
Grateful much, are we!
Mother Nature craves for attention,
Yet us the ignorant teenagers
Shut her out,
See beyond those brick walls,
You have encapsulated yourselves in,
There's a blossoming world,
Where yonder yellow sun glows,
Just run and capture the crusty horizon!

# Embarrassed

Flushed face, tinted cheeks,
Salty eyes prickling with tears,
Parted lips,
with doe-y eyes
caught in headlights,
Rebellious mind refuses to tame,
Reputation crushed,
returning home with poker face,
Bleeding heart,
Dejected much,
And walls breaking down,
Oh, why couldn't people forget,
The wonderful play,
Of my heart being trampled before them?

# <u>Slandered One</u>

The flood broke the walls down,
The secrets behind those bricks,
Came tumbling down,
Bashed, hit and bruised,
Had encountered it all,
But repute needed to hold on,
"Stay strong!" it exclaimed,
The cold wall was cracking in pain,
One could only take that much toll!
Then came the hardest blow of them all,
Bricks and cement definitely couldn't take no more,
Out came the flow,
The last barrier had been crossed,
The walls declared, my bricks reported,
"Gush over and out!"

# Felon

Pointing fingers at an unfortunate one,
Who wasn't the convict
To this crime,
Tears out of those droopy eyes,
Wounds start to
etch on her moldable heart,
Why her?
She might never know,
Didn't ask for anything that wasn't hers,
Nor wanted,
yet life had cruel plans in store,
Her potion to her wound,
A blossoming muse,
Of nature's gleam!

# Need or Want?

The strongest and wittiest of them all
That has ever lived, homo sapiens!
We are ever so weird.
Material is something
That everyone tends to cherish,
But isn't it amusing
Material is the fastest to perish,
Abstract of all kinds
Stay until the last,
Till death do us part,
Hypocritical lots we are
Indeed, so very absurd,
Are the workings
Of this wondrous world!

# Mask

All smiles we are to
the ones with power,
All frowns we reveal to the ones
with empty arms extended,
Befitting masks to be adorned
for every being we come across,
just as fast as we shed tears
for misfortunes faced by each one of us.
All possess a sob story of their own,
But look down upon the other who own,
Their treasure's brimming,
The questions we seek answers to,
Don't seem to lie within our reach,
Comes with a huge price,
Much alike to the cursed Pandora's box!

# Mirage

How alluring is the scent of a perfect life,
Concocted by the goddess herself,
Eager are we to take possession,
Not much for the ones in oppression,
The drive of desire blinds us all,
Working and disassembling setbacks in the way,
Ah, we have crossed that finish line,
*mon ami*, have a seat now,
Let's take that quick rendezvous as planned,
Let's grab something,
Hold on a minute dear,
What's that I hear,
"Click-click, bang!"
It closes with a shock,
Deceived and heartbroken,
We sit like a sullen rock,
As realization sets in,
The cage glimmers with a flashy bling,
Dusty and dingy on the inside,
What was its description,
Oh, how naive are we,
It's a golden mirage of frustration!

# The Mighty Coward

Hail to us! The mighty beings,
ruling the Earth for innumerable centuries,
Species after species,
we have conquered,
The throne of might,
is rightfully ours.
We proclaim ourselves to be king to all,
as nature cowers in fear,
in burrows and holes,
nurturing themselves,
they fend in fright,
as they look upon their homes,
so savagely taken,
set ablaze they are.
And here we sing tales of
honor and valor,
when ironically,
we are to shatter!
When no other shall let
another of its own to suffer,
when the "wild",

have ethics and manners,
Here we are the mighty beings,
Letting millions of our own to bleed to grief!

# <u>Plunge</u>

Serene and calm,
the reflection of the waves,
soothe the onlooker from afar,
as he watches the dance,
playing out in front of him,
an actor is what its named,
The ocean and its mysterious ways.
For it may grieve and dance,
all at once,
like a monotone force.
He wants to be one,
with the curious liquid as
it flows throughout the shore,
kissing the damp sand,
where his feet meet the swaying waters.
In he goes to take a deep dive,
as the cold starts to chill his spine.
Numbness engulfs him,
as he sets to swim back home,
but the dark thunder abruptly sounds,
Stretching out its arms to drown
him in its deadly hug.

War ensues as man and ocean,
fight their very best against one another,
And out comes the ocean victorious,
Soon the dark clouds assemble to celebrate,
and toast glum to rollick.

52

# Longing

Turning the pages of the memory book of mankind,
tragedy isn't afar,
our once home is described to be,
a precedent oasis of paradise.
Throughout the silent echoes,
of the void ether of unknown,
Intelligent creatures, ha!
We proclaim ourselves to be,
the only life who thrived,
comical isn't it,
our trivial little title,
built upon the trickling remnants,
of our slaughtered fellow tenants,
as we readily set
our first abode ablaze!
The fake bubble,
we construct,
a temporary respite,
nowhere near gratifying
It shall and will burst soon!
As we look upon our once flourishing home,
become deserted and alone!

# Insensitive

Say all you want,
to that dainty soul,
it doesn't matter,
bitter or cold.
Shatter her all you want,
till she morphs into a tattered one,
bruise and vent
all that anger that you pent
in your rickety tent.
She'll heal and break and heal that
fragile heart all over again!
"Worthless and useless,"
chant all you want,
but all must admit,
she is a survivor,
No intended taunt!
Out comes her savior,
one fine sunny day,
Bellows in a certain gruff way,
"Oh, you imbeciles!" he scoffs,
"You are all one of a kind.
Just like pieces of paper,

being torn and blown away,
your words are such a metaphor!"
Your words intended for yourselves.
You all bow down in utter shame,
as you see the turtle,
emerge from her rock-hard shell,
Ravishly metamorphosed into one of the rarest kinds.

# Goodbyes

Those last mumbles,
of your kindred one,
echoes through your mind,
like a haunting conundrum.
First comes shock,
then sweeps over the courtesy,
of the much-anticipated grief.
Confused is one indeed!
The dam of sorrow shatters through your walls,
like an eerie flood,
just waiting to wash out!
As the fluid chills through,
like a never-ending bath,
lost memories are relived again,
with a mellowed smile.
A projector ingrained,
flickering of the love,
It's a horrific chase.
Then comes acceptance knocking on your door,
One yells, "This is a maze
I want to run from!"
Then that lost ghostly voice,

Of your heart whispers in a feeble tone,
"Banishing the ghostly love,
Won't help you heal,
Oh, tender-hearted one!"

# Numb

Bravery, gallantry and boldness,
What a lovely array of words,
Brilliant attributes they are indeed,
To show off as medals of pride,
Pinned are those pieces of metal,
Upon their heavily embellished…!
"What?" you may ask,
"Suits, of course!" I exclaim.
Dive and magnify,
their hearts,
Expect to see heaps of good earns,
"Huh! What a waste," you murmur,
Their hearts, oh so chilling,
No emotion,
Almost a statue frosted.
Erected upon the
marvelous bosom of ego.
No tears, no pain,
A mantra resounding in their brains!
Branded as valor,
But now you know,
Deep inside,

Their incapability, their incapacity,
Of opening up their solemn heart,
and letting their dams break,
Only an act of cowardice!

59

# Breaking the Broken

Screws and rods,
Fitted in place,
Supporting the broken rods of steel,
Soon they too shall get misplaced,
Dissembling that building,
They're so lovingly made.
Madam! Urgent attention required,
a case of ICU, Sir,
…make sure your tools are in place!
We must execute plan B,
It is the most appropriate one,
reconstruction must be in place.
Mold the steel,
Get that iron hammer,
For we shall shatter this structure,
Fix that fracture,
And build a finer one!

# Crystal

She was a saint on Earth,
Looked up by all around her,
Unhinged and unbroken,
Pure was the state
of inner mind,
Not one scar resided,
Not one etch of a bruise,
Pain, an absolute foreigner
To the young one there.
Not once did it burn,
Or was forced in a furnace,
Or flooded by the
breaking of the internal dams,
Was that heart all golden?
I am in a dilemma of course!
Oh, this description,
is all but a sham,
For not one crystalline soul,
Has walked this lane of life,
Without a permanent etch of hurt!

# Isn't?

Rapidly comes knocking,
Your terrible nightmare,
oh dear!
Setbacks and obstacles,
Success's kindred ones,
All eager to soil,
Bang!
there goes…
your sculpture of blood, sweat and tears,
Boom!
There closes the portals
to your world of dreams,
Shut!
Shatters the windows of possibilities,
A sly smirk rests on their wicked faces,
This is your fear thriving indeed!
Here comes the waterworks,
Building in your eyes,
But they pay no heed,
Definitely not kind!
Your structure floods,
With their merry chuckles,

They turn towards you,
Expecting you to cower,
Oh, they were close,
But you shatter their aghast faces,
With a smug snigger,
"My darlings,
It is what it is,
It isn't what it isn't!"

# **<u>Turn Around</u>**

When fear comes knocking,
On your stout lil' door,
You think it's easier,
To show your back,
then to turn around.
When life bombards you,
With consecutive power bombs,
You think it's easier to shield yourself,
then to face and turn around.
When life takes a turn,
Down the rough rocky lane,
You feel it's effortless to
reverse your way around.
Start looking closer,
Realization dawns,
Your fear may bring love,
and your bombardment uncover treasure,
Your rugged lane might just gift you a smooth ride
to a blissful life!

# Stay

There its stands,
Tall and mighty in front of you,
Your biggest nemesis in the ring,
Yourself and you.
Throwing jab after jab of obstacles,
Hook of challenges,
Punch of setbacks,
And knockout of situations,
You blackout on yourself,
You fail to understand,
How do you stab yourself,
Right in the back,
With gashes of wounds in red,
It indeed leaves you in a mess.
That phantom of a coach,
Whispers in an encouraging voice,
"Get up! You have coached yourself
enough, my child.
Now fight the real game,
And prove your might!"
You open your eyes,
To see a new opponent,

Clad in black,
As you realize you were,
Just a rookie,
In the ring of life!

# **<u>Perspective Through Perception</u>**

Limbs incapacitated,
thunder rumbles in an audible growl,
tears furiously tumbling down
the quaint little face,
Wishing to yourself that you could,
Mute all that,
Cowering away in the gloom,
Of your dark and sullen room.
You think to yourself,
What all you could do,
If you had your life
under your grasp!
"Close your eyes,"
A voice resounds in your head,
"Let your emotions seep through."
You follow the mystery voice
in a desperate attempt,
to make all those noises dissipate,
Soon you find yourself,
becoming more sore inside.
You let your dam break through,
Allow yourself to dampen like a burst balloon,

You find yourself exploding,
Like a ticking bomb,
Your mind mining,
For the right solace.
You see the key lies right in front of you.
You open your somber eyes,
And see the booming thunder turn to dulcet pitter-patters of
the rain,
Your limbs' confinement fallen apart,
As you run out to the moist fields,
You realize and let out a dramatic sigh,
Seeing it was only a treacherous game of perspective and
perceptions!

9 789948 775843